Queen Elizabeth II

A Biography of Queen Elizabeth II

Table of Contents

Introduction

Thank you for taking the time to pick up this book documenting the life of Queen Elizabeth II.

This book serves as a biography of Queen Elizabeth II and the incredible life that she lives. Currently, Elizabeth II is the longest reigning Queen in the history of the United Kingdom. She has lived and ruled through many different periods, and to this day continues to be largely respected by the people of Britain.

This biography will educate you on Queen Elizabeth II's life, from her childhood, to the unlikely circumstances that led to her becoming the Queen, through to her many challenges and victories as the ruler of the United Kingdom.

This book discusses the most pivotal moments in the Queen's life, along with what her incredible legacy will be.

Once again, thanks for choosing this book, I hope you find it to be insightful and enjoyable!

Chapter 1: Family and Early Life

Elizabeth Alexandra Mary was born into the royal family on the 21st of April in the year 1926. Her father, who was at the time called Prince Albert, Duke of York, was the second son of King George V. Her mother, Elizabeth **Angela Marguerite Bowes-Lyon,** was from a family of Scottish aristocracy and had improved her family's position in the society greatly by marrying the man who later became the King himself. But no one could have imagined that at the time. In fact, when Prince Albert first proposed to her, she refused. She was being courted by another royal man, and it was only through Prince Albert's persistence and a visit from his mother, then the Queen of England, that the Princess agreed to marry him. And although this Prince Albert was quite important, he was never meant to be the King, that honor went to his older brother Edward. When she was born to Edward and Elizabeth, the young Princess who would become Queen Elizabeth II could not have known she would one day be the Queen.

From the moment of her birth, Elizabeth II was groomed and trained for her future role as a royal woman, and as far as anyone could tell, she took to it very naturally. She grew up with great wealth, living in beautiful estates and surrounded by some of the most powerful people in the world. And although being around these extraordinary people must have rubbed off on her, she seemed to be born with a natural talent for her role. Even the great Winston Churchill noticed that she seemed to give off "an air of authority" when she was still just an infant child. However, it was not obvious until much later in her life that she would one day be Queen, that was left up to fate itself.

Elizabeth has always lived a life of great privilege, having for instance been educated by a Governess that came to live at their family home. She was known as a happy young girl who liked very much to play with the dogs and other animals that her family kept at their estate. Even as a child she was reserved, and properly royal in the way that she conducted herself. When the young Elizabeth was only four years old, her sister Princess Margaret was born. They grew up together and were very close to each other, spending most of their time together and in the company of their closest family members. Their mother personally oversaw their education and raised the two sisters in a tightly knit nuclear family. The people of the United Kingdom saw them as a symbol of the ideal family and looked up to them as models of the ideals valued by the Anglican Church, in which the King of England is the highest leader.

Elizabeth, who called herself "Lilibet" as a child, was also quite close to and a favorite of her grandfather George Frederick Ernest. This grandfather was the man known as King George V of the United Kingdom and had been ruling since 1910. When Elizabeth was born, her grandfather was already 60 years of age and sadly he died just ten years later in 1936. King George V was injured fighting in World War I many years before, having been thrown from a horse in France. George was a heavy smoker and a somewhat adventurous man, two aspects that contributed to his health problems. He had recurring breathing issues and many different illnesses for decades before his eventual death.

Her grandfather's reign was very significant because the empire he ruled over, and the whole world for that matter, went through many changes during his time as King. Before World War I, the vast majority of Europe, and even Russia, was ruled by monarchs. Not only that, but most of them were related to each other by blood through some type of family connection. This familial interconnection of the royal families of Europe was a practice dating back to the Medieval era. Intermarriage was the way in which peace was maintained in Europe because it was believed that any sensible King would not want to make war with his own family members! And with only a few exceptions, such as France, the majority of Europe was still under some type of monarchy.

Much of this changed by the end of World War I since many monarchs had been overthrown by different revolutions across Europe and Russia. In addition to this turmoil, Irish Nationalists were fighting the United Kingdom's government for their independence from England and from the control of the King. Across the empire that the King controlled, colonies like India were starting to follow in the footsteps of the United States and demand their independence from the King as well.

Parliament, similar to the Senate and House of Representatives in the United States, was also starting to disagree with the King and pushed back against certain policies, much more than they had in previous time periods. This was the beginning of the era of decolonization and the continued waning of the power of the monarchy in the United Kingdom and Europe.

It was in this uncertain world that King George V passed away in 1936. His son Edward VIII became King shortly thereafter, but would only reign for less than one year. Edward VIII was in love with a woman named Wallis Simpson, who was already married but in the process of having a divorce. To make things worse, this was her second divorce and she was an American by birth. Although it was legal to divorce at that time, it was not socially acceptable in the United Kingdom. This was largely due to the fact that divorce was considered a sin by the Church of England. Edward VIII proposed that he marry her anyway but not name her Queen so that she had no power or claim to the throne, or possibly even the wealth of the royal family at all. The other parts of the government of the United Kingdom did not accept this idea. It was thought that this move could create a crisis because it would have required massive changes to the way in which royal succession worked. Edward VIII was forced to choose what to do next, and although no one could stop him from marrying her and still being the King, he chose to maintain his honor and his love for Simpson. Just eleven months into his reign, Edward VIII gave up the throne and married the woman he loved. This was basically an unheard of move for a King, but was greatly fortunate for the future Queen Elizabeth II. Also, it was a rather ironic turn of events for the Church of England. In 1534, the Church of England was formed when King Henry VIII broke away from the Roman Catholic Church precisely because he wanted to divorce his wife, and the Catholic Church forbid it. This turn of events illustrates how much power the monarchy of England had lost up to this time; once a King would form a whole new church to get divorced but now the King would have to step down just because his wife was divorced herself! That said, it is hard to think of a more touching way to show your love for someone than to give up control of the biggest empire in the world.

It was only by this very rare and unusual occurrence that Elizabeth's father became King George VI. If this had not happened, King Edward VIII could have stayed in power, married a different woman, and the children they had together would have been next in line for the throne. If things went this way, Elizabeth would almost certainly never have become the Queen of England. With her father taking the throne, the path of Elizabeth's life had just changed dramatically. Imagine the excitement of a ten-year-old girl who has just found out she could one day be the Queen of her own empire. But this is just the beginning of the adventure that was young Elizabeth's life, because by the time she turned just twelve years old, the world was starting to face the aggression of Germany under the fascist rule of Adolf Hitler. It was during these uncertain and harsh years that the young Princess would begin to grow into the role she would later embody as a leader of her people.

Chapter 2: Journey to the Throne

Throughout the second world war, the young queen-to-be never really left England, even when her home city of London was being bombed by the Nazi forces. During the war, young Elizabeth's royal parents became stalwart symbols of the resistance against fascism, with her mother being called "the most dangerous woman in Europe" by none other than Adolf Hitler himself. Though she was still young during these years of turmoil, she did not shy away from her role as a leader and was already acting much more like an adult than a child. She and her sister Margaret had to hide out not far from London, sometimes suffering through nights so cold that a glass of water would freeze as it sat next to their beds. At just 13 years old, she met her future husband Phillip, at which point she said she fell in love with him as they began to exchange letters. When she was just 14, she gave a BBC radio address to the children of her country who had been evacuated due to Nazi bombing campaigns. The next year, she was named a colonel-in-chief of the British Army. And by the time she was about to turn 18, the government changed the laws so that she could act in the place of her father, the King, when he was unavailable. This honor is called "Counsellor of State" and gave the young Princess a great deal of responsibility. For the rest of the war, she served as a statesman and a symbol of hope for her people. In this period, she began to accompany her parents on official visits, learning how to act and what was expected of a royal person in her role. She also served actively in the armed forces, and although she was not sent into battle, she was trained as a mechanic and driver of military trucks and other vehicles, such as ambulances. When the war ended, she and her younger sister Margaret put on plain clothes and celebrated the victory alongside her people, hoping that no one would recognize them. It seems that they succeeded, with everyone so relieved that the war was over, the two Princesses slipped by unnoticed.

Maybe it was the war, maybe it was luck, maybe it was the foresight of her parents, but giving this sort of responsibility and power to a young Princess was a less than normal occurrence. At this point in time, the Princess was next in line for the throne.

However, if her parents had had a son at any point, he would have jumped ahead of her in the line of succession. That said, it seems Elizabeth was asked to play the role of both a Prince and Princess. She was asked to support her people in spirit, as a Princess, and lead in state affairs, like a Prince. Throughout these early formative years, Elizabeth embraced her role as a ruler-to-be and shined even through these dark years of the Great War. And although not a wholly new idea by any stretch of the imagination, giving this sort of responsibility to a woman in the 1940s was a sure sign that attitudes were changing about the role and place of women in society. By having a high profile and important royal woman treated this way, a strong signal would have been sent to the population, which surely played to be a huge inspiration to women in the United Kingdom and all over the world.

Within two years of the war ending, Elizabeth was engaged to her future husband Phillip Mountbatten, a Greek and Danish royal who is both Elizabeth's third cousin and second cousin once removed. If that sounds strange, it is helpful to remember that the royal families of Europe had been intermarrying for hundreds of years, and nearly every royal person in Europe has some relation to each other. This practice of intermarriage is also why Phillip, who comes from a German family, could have been born in Greece, hold titles in Greece and Denmark, be educated in France, the United Kingdom, and Germany, and serve in the Royal Navy of the United Kingdom. And although Phillip is undoubtedly a royal person, many members of Elizabeth's own family and others in the government doubted if he was "royal enough".

From the perspective of the royal court of England, Phillip's family was less than desirable. Although Phillip used the name Mountbatten, he is actually a member of the House of Glücksburg. The house he comes from has ruled before, such as in Denmark from the mid-1400s until now. They also ruled Greece from the late 1800s until the monarchy was abolished in the 1970s. And they took the throne of Norway in 1905, which they still hold to this day. All of this sounds impressive, but the complication is that Phillip was living in the United Kingdom in part because his family was exiled from Greece due to conflict in

1917. Phillip's father, Prince Andrew of Greece and Denmark, was an important military leader in the Greek war against Turkey. Many people blamed his decisions for the loss of that war to the Turkish in 1922. This unfortunate family history tarred Phillip's name by some degree.

But this may not have been the biggest problem with Phillip from the viewpoint of the British royal court. Phillip's mother, Princess Alice of Battenberg, was deaf and schizophrenic at a time when both of those things were considered very shameful. But to make things worse, Phillip's family members were living under the name Mountbatten, as a way to hide their history as a family of German descent. When World War I started, the family changed their name to show they were loyal to England, and many of the men served in the British military. Even though they had served England for many years already, and helped to defeat the Nazi government in World War II, the people of England were distrustful and very suspicious of anyone with a connection to Germany at all. Of course, a royal family can not keep their history a secret, because all marriages and family relations are well recorded and known to anyone who looks at the records. As a result of this, many people in the royal court of Elizabeth's family voiced their concerns about this German connection openly. What may have saved Phillip, at least from too much negative pressure, is that fact that he served in the Navy of the United Kingdom. He fought against the Nazi forces, had been schooled for part of his life in England, and by any measure was a citizen of the United Kingdom, at least by the time that the two were to marry. He had lived most of his life in the United Kingdom at this point and had left his home of Greece at such a young age that he could only understand a little bit of the Greek language. It would be hard for anyone to seriously question where his loyalties were placed.

Yet there was another (possibly worse) concern that some had about Phillip as well. Many believed that Phillip was being controlled by his uncle Admiral Louis Mountbatten. This man was a high-ranking member of the United Kingdom's military, and the Governor-General of India, among many other titles. He would later become the longest serving leader of the British armed forces ever. The Admiral was a member of Phillip's mother's family. Many distrusted him, and not only because of his German ancestry. The man was seen as very ambitious, interested in gaining power for himself, and therefore a threat to many people in the government of the United Kingdom. Some believed that the Admiral would use his nephew, Prince Phillip, to manipulate the heads of state to serve his own needs. Some of these fears might be evidenced by the fact that Mountbatten had pushed for the royal family to be renamed the House of Mountbatten when the royals were married. This did not happen, partially due to pressure from Winston Churchill, and Elizabeth's family retained the name House of Windsor. The Admiral was a mentor to and huge influence on the life of Prince Phillip, and later was a mentor to his son Prince Charles. In fact, it was the Admiral who arranged the first meeting between Elizabeth and her future husband. Maybe it runs in her blood, but none of this doubt or pressure would stop Elizabeth from marrying the man that she chose, and the one that she loved.

They were engaged and quickly married in 1947 when Elizabeth was 21 years old. They would have done so sooner, but the King had only given Phillip permission to marry his daughter if they waited until she was 21 years old to become engaged formally. And although he was marrying into a great position in the society, this move was not one without sacrifice for the Prince. Phillip had to renounce his titles as Prince of Greece and Denmark to avoid a conflict of interest. He also had to leave the Greek Orthodox Church, which he was born into, and convert officially to the Church of England. This second requirement was not such a challenge for Phillip because he already had been attending services at the Church of England for many years at this time. And, although he gained prestige and power through this marriage, Phillip knew that he could never be the King of England or the ruler of any other country. Because of the way royal succession works in England, when a King marries a woman she will become Queen, as one would expect. However, when a Queen marries a man, he simply becomes Consort of the Queen. The children they have together become the heirs to the throne, but there is no way in which the Consort of the Queen can become the King. This is why Phillip remained a Prince even after Elizabeth became the Queen. And although he was and is still called "Prince", he is not technically a royal Prince because he has renounced his royal titles to Greece and Denmark, and has no claim to the throne of England.

After the marriage, Prince Phillip was named Duke of Edinburgh, a title that he holds to this day. And although the wedding went very well, it was not without some controversy and hardship. Due to the anti-German sentiment at the time, Phillip's German family members were not invited to the wedding at all. This included his sisters, all of whom married German royalty with connections to the failed Nazi government. Elizabeth's own uncle was also not invited, the man who had given up his birthright as the King of England, because he was still considered too disgraced to be allowed at such an event. And Elizabeth herself had to pay for her wedding dress with wartime rations, reflecting the still harsh conditions in the country at that time. With all of that said, the royal wedding was very much a momentous occasion, with more than 200 million people listening to the BBC Radio coverage of the event all over the globe.

In the very next year of 1948, Princess Elizabeth gave birth to a son, Prince Charles, who has been next in line for the throne since his mother became Queen. Prince Charles was born at Buckingham Palace in London, the main residence and headquarters for the royal family since the 1800s. Like his mother, and most upper-class children, he was privately educated at his family home by a woman called a governess, who specializes in teaching children. But this only lasted until he was roughly eight years old, at which point he started to attend a private school. This was an unusual move for a royal family member but must have been seen as a progressive and modern decision. Placing him in a school like this would have removed some of the typical separation that royal children experience from other children their age, and from the world around them. The Admiral Mountbatten, who was a big influence on Prince Philip, played a large role in the life of Prince Charles as well. The Prince even referred to his grand uncle as his "Honorary Grandfather" and he served as mentor to the Prince until the Admiral died in 1959.

In the year 1950, the couple had their first and only daughter who they named Princess Anne. Princess Anne was born at Clarence House, another royal home in London, and followed a similar educational path as her elder brother. At first, she was tutored by a governess, but then attended private schools alongside other children. Later in her life, the Princess would go on to be the first British royal person to compete in the Olympics, using her great talent for horseback riding.

By 1951, King George VI was frequently too ill to make public appearances and Princess Elizabeth would often stand in his place. She was even traveling to meet with world leaders on his behalf. On the sixth of February 1952, King George VI passed away in his sleep, having battled cancer and many other ailments for several years. Prince Phillip heard the news first and told his wife about her father's death while they were on a trip to their home in Kenya. They rushed back to England as soon as possible because it was now time for the Princess to become Queen. At this time, there was some controversy over how the family of the new monarch would be called. Elizabeth comes from the House of Windsor. Her husband comes from the House of Mountbatten. Normally, the house name of the male would be used when a new monarch is crowned. This would mean that England would go from being ruled by the House of Windsor to being ruled by the House of Mountbatten. But Elizabeth's mother, and other prominent figures like Winston Churchill, rejected this idea and pushed for the name Windsor to continue to rule England. The queen-to-be obliged, even though Prince Phillip complained that he was the only man in the United Kingdom that was not allowed to give his own name to his own children.

The coronation of Queen Elizabeth II took fourteen months to plan. Many committees and councils were formed to organize what would be the first ever coronation to be televised. On the second day of June 1953, Princess Elizabeth was presented with St. Edward's Crown, which has been used in every coronation since it was made in the year 1661. The crown is formed from gold, set with exactly 444 stones, and weighs just under five pounds. Elizabeth swore a holy oath to uphold the law and to lead the Church of England, as had her father before her. Then, at just 25 years of age, she became Queen Elizabeth II of the United Kingdom, Canada, Australia, New Zealand, Barbados, the Bahamas, Papua New Guinea, Solomon Islands, Belize, Grenada, Tuvalu, Saint Vincent and the Grenadines, Saint Lucia, Antigua and Barbuda, Saint Kitts and Nevis, and Jamaica. She also became the leader of the Commonwealth of Nations, a group of nations that were once British colonies and territories. On this momentous day, Queen Elizabeth became the head of state for a vast group of nations and territories, nearly sixty countries that span across every continent. This even includes a territory in Antarctica that is used mainly for scientific research. The coronation kicked off what has become the longest reign of a queen in British history. On the sixth of February 2017, Queen Elizabeth celebrated her Sapphire Jubilee, which commemorates 65 years on the throne. In these next chapters, we will discuss the ups and down of these incredible 65 years, and the vast legacy that this unique Queen has left to the world.

Chapter 3: The First Twenty Years (1952-1972)

As one of her very first acts as Queen, Elizabeth and her husband took a seven-month-long trip in which they visited thirteen different countries. It was a somewhat unique move to go amongst her people, to physically visit them, and later even shake their hands. In fact, she was the very first monarch of Australia and New Zealand to visit either of those countries. The crowds that she drew were very large, with some estimating that 75% of the people of Australia gathered to see her in person during her visit there. And although she is and was very popular, this Queen has chosen to be reserved about her views on politics, choosing to focus heavily on her role as a symbolic and even spiritual leader of her people. When Queen Elizabeth II reflected on her life in the 1980s, she said that she did not have a proper mentorship before taking the throne. She believed herself to be too young and that her father died too suddenly to prepare for her role as Queen. But, she also said that one must accept what life gives them and rise to the circumstances. As far as anyone can tell, she did exactly that and did so very well. With that said, the changing nature of England's role in its' colonies and Commonwealth territories created many challenges for the new Queen to face.

Across the United Kingdom and the Commonwealth territories, there was a growing current of "republicanism". This is not referring to a conservative political party as it does in the United States, but rather to a movement to reform the government from being a constitutional monarchy to being a republic. In other words, to remove all the power of the monarchy and give it to the elected representatives of the people, such as the system of government in France or the United States of America. In many ways, the constitutional monarchy was already like this, with non-royal officials running the majority of the government. However, in some cases, it is still possible for the monarch to intervene, such as appointing new ministers, pushing an official to reign, or even formally dismissing a government official, such as a Prime Minister. And although the monarch still has a decent amount of power, they are only supposed to act on the advice of the Prime Minister and other members of the government. To understand how this anti-monarchy feeling came to be, it is helpful to learn a little about the history of monarchy in England.

In 1642, England experienced a civil war after King Charles I ruled heavy-handedly and without input from the non-royal parts of the government. He unilaterally imposed taxes, which many believed were very unfair in their nature. This led to the complete overthrow of the monarchy for a short period. Then in 1660, the monarchy was restored but not without serious tensions and controversy. By 1688, a group of people who believed that Parliament should rule, so that the will of the people would be the rule of law, overthrew the King again and in the next year created a Bill of Rights that placed the power of Parliament above the monarchy. This was essentially the beginning of the constitutional monarchy in its modern form. From here on out in the United Kingdom, the monarch is still the head of state on paper but is seriously limited by the Parliament, which is supposed to represent the interests of the people they govern. For the most part, this compromise worked, but as time went on there were always people who wanted to lessen the power of the monarchy or take the monarchy away altogether. This became especially true during the new Queen's reign, as many colonies and territories gained independence from England or transitioned away from the rule of the Queen by becoming Commonwealth Nations.

In 1956, the Queen faced her first crisis and the first major moment in which she had to use her power as a monarch. Israeli and Egyptian forces were clashing in the Egyptian Sinai area. The militaries of Britain and France issued a ceasefire order which was ignored by both sides. The conflict grew as fighting escalated. British and French forces became involved in the conflict by landing troops in the area, and started to push the Egyptian army back with the goal of retaking the Suez Canal. This canal was historically controlled by Britain and France, but is located in Egypt. Fearing a further escalation of the conflict, the United Nations, the USSR, and the United States pressured Britain and France to withdraw. U.S. President Dwight D.

Eisenhower had even threatened that the economy of the United Kingdom could be ruined if they did not pull out of Egypt. The whole mess became an embarrassment to Britain, some believing it signaled the end of the United Kingdom as a major force of global power.

Because the Queen does not make her political views known publicly, it is usually difficult to know what she believes on any specific issue. According to the Prime Minister of Britain at the time, Sir Anthony Eden, the Queen was in favor of the military actions in Egypt. However, the Queen's uncle, Admiral Mountbatten, said that the Queen was opposed to the intervention in the first place. Either way, the scandal reflected most heavily on Prime Minister Eden, who resigned in disgrace two months after this episode. It was now time for the Queen to exercise one of her royal duties, appointing a new Prime Minister. The Queen consulted with Ministers, Lords, and even Winston Churchill about who should be named next. She followed their advice and named Harold MacMillan as the new Prime Minister. This decision was favored by many, but others criticized the decision on the grounds that it did not reflect the will of the people.

In 1957, the Queen visited the United States and made her first speech in front of the United Nations in New York City. In that speech, she celebrated the independence of Commonwealth Nations that were once colonies under the control of the very monarchy that she embodies. She expressed her hope that the common ideals and interests of these nations would unite them toward a more peaceful world. This speech is indicative of her general attitude toward the winding down of the British Empire, as more and more former colonies turned into independent nations. On a tour of Asian and African countries in 1961, she stood alongside President Kwame Nkrumah of Ghana, who had just replaced her as the leader of that country, seeming to embrace this shift of power in a peaceful and elegant fashion. She did not shy away from the trip, even though both she and President Nkrumah were likely targets for assassination in that country.

The year before this, in 1960, she had given birth again, this time to Prince Andrew. Other than missing a Parliamentary opening ceremony, the pregnancy did not seem to slow her down at all. The then Prime Minister Harold MacMillan wrote of the Queen that she has "the heart and stomach of a man", but he forgot to mention that she still had the grace and poise of a proper woman as well. In 1964, she gave birth to a third son, Prince Edward who was her final child.

The time of Prime Minister Harold MacMillan came to an end in 1963. The Greek Cypriots of Cyprus fought a guerrilla war against British forces and gained independence in 1960. In the years of 1960 to 1963, Nigeria, Southern Cameroon, British Somalia (later Somalia), Sierra Leone, Tanganyika (later Tanzania), Trinidad and Tobago, Uganda, and Kenya all gained independence from Britain. All of these nations worked with Britain to become independent in an orderly way that did not negatively affect the United Kingdom. Though seen as a loss by some, the majority of these nations stayed in the Commonwealth, meaning they govern themselves but maintain some ties to the Queen. With some of his strategies failing and confidence in him declining, MacMillan had survived a vote by Parliament to keep him as Prime Minister by just a single vote. After this, MacMillan became very ill with prostate cancer, and it was clear that he should resign.

This meant it was again time for the Queen to appoint a new Prime Minister. It seems that she followed MacMillan's sole advice to appoint Alec Douglas-Home. This was an unpopular move, however, because MacMillan was disgraced and many thought it was not right to appoint a Prime Minister based on a single person's opinion. Just two years later, in 1965, the Conservative party changed the conventional way of doing things, such that the Parliament would essentially choose the Prime Minister and the Queen would simply approve their choice. The Queen still has the final say in the matter and can also dismiss the Prime Minister whenever she feels the need to do so. This is also the case for all of the Queen's colonies.

In 1965, Rhodesia declared independence from Britain unilaterally. This was the first time that a colony formally and completely broke away from Britain since the United States declared independence in 1776. The Queen dismissed their Prime Minister, Ian Smith, but being that they no longer recognized British rule, he continued to govern for many years after that. The international community generally considered these actions to be illegal, and they followed up by imposing sanctions on Rhodesia. In 1966, Barbados followed in the footsteps of Jamaica from just a few years earlier and kicked off the process of independence in the Caribbean that would last into the 1980s. Again, most of these were peaceful movements that worked with Britain to gain self-governance. The process of independence for the British territories in the Pacific also began in this period, with Fiji gaining its independence in 1970.

Even with the uncertainty of some many colonies becoming independent, the Queen enjoyed high approval ratings and great popularity within the United Kingdom. In the year 1970, the Queen introduced a brand new tradition that is very much in line with her personality as a Queen of the people. While touring Australia and New Zealand, she created a practice known as the "royal walkabout". During a walkabout, the Queen, or another royal person, walks amongst her people, sometimes shaking hands, and speaking to them face-to-face. This is a very significant way to show the humanity of the Queen. In past times the whole royal family would have likely kept themselves very separate from the common people, and even laughed at the idea of physically touching them. This was never the attitude of Queen Elizabeth II. In the next 28 years of her life, we will see a Queen lead her people through a rapidly changing world, a whirlwind of different crises, and come out the over side with a bright smile and the pose of a truly seasoned leader.

Chapter 4: Queen in a Changing World (1972-2000)

As we have already seen from the first 25 years of the Queen's reign, the power of the United Kingdom was waning as the British empire was winding down, and it seemed necessary for the United Kingdom to increase ties with the rest of Europe. After many negotiations, the United Kingdom formally joined the European Community in 1973. The European Community, which later became known as the European Union, was the first attempt to integrate the economies of the various countries in Europe into a single market. The idea was that such integration would prevent war between European nations and allow Europe to stand unified against the Soviet Union. Gaining entry into the organization was a significant victory for the United Kingdom, in part because they had been trying to join the organization since 1961. The European Community President had vetoed their membership based on the fear that they would bring the influence of the United States into the organization. Later, there were also some concerns about the United Kingdom's relationship with its' Commonwealth Nations. Though the United Kingdom has been a member since 1973, they have always maintained a somewhat detached relationship with the European Community. The United Kingdom has chosen to keep their own identity separate from that of the rest of Europe. This was a major theme of the Queen's role as a leader through these many years of change: to keep up with and adapt to a shifting world, while managing to maintain the strong identity of the United Kingdom as an independent nation.

In the year before this, the undercurrent of anti-monarchy was coming to a head within the United Kingdom, with an event that came to be known as the Bloody Sunday of 1972. Protestors in Northern Ireland, which is part of the United Kingdom, were peacefully assembled to push for Irish self-governance and the reunion of the island, which is to this day split between Northern Ireland (UK) and the independent Republic of Ireland. British soldiers shot 26 civilians with their service rifles, leading to the deaths of fourteen of the protestors.

Although the British government did investigate, the report they published failed to hold the soldiers or their officers responsible for their actions, at least in any meaningful way. This lead to increased support for the radical, violent separatist movement known as the Irish Republican Army. The group known as the IRA was formed a few years earlier in reaction to the deployment of British troops in Northern Ireland. This was done in order to contain riots that stemmed from an initially peaceful civil rights movement that pushed for the equal treatment of Irish Catholics in the United Kingdom. It is helpful here to remember that the Queen is the head of the Church of England, a protestant church that formed when King Henry VIII broke away from the Catholic church in 1534. The conflict with the IRA was just heating up in the United Kingdom, a conflict that would come to affect the Queen and her family on a very personal level.

By 1974, the government of Prime Minister Edward Heath was losing support and the Queen was asked to call a parliamentary election. The election was essentially tied, known as a "hung parliament". Heath resigned after this and the Queen appointed Harold Wilson as the next Prime Minister. They likely picked him because of his experience, as he had already served as Prime Minister from 1964-1970. On the heels of this shake-up at home, Australia experienced a crisis of even larger proportions in 1975. Often referred to simply as "the Dismissal", or the Australian constitutional crisis, this event called into question Australia's relationship with the monarchy as its true ruler. The issue at hand was the dismissal of Australian Prime Minister Gough Whitlam by Governor-General Sir John Kerr. The Governor-General is the official representative of the Queen in a country where she is the monarch. This dates back to the time when it would have taken months or weeks to even pass a message to the monarch from one of their colonies. Essentially, when the Queen is not in Australia, the Governor-General acts in her place. After some deliberation and the refusal of the Prime Minister to cooperate with demands and exceptions made of him, Governor-General Kerr formally dismissed Whitlam. This led immediately to angry protests from the public, who viewed this move as a huge over-stepping of the power of the monarchy. The Queen was asked to reverse the decision, as she is the only person in the world who legally could, but refused to become involved on the grounds that the actions were legal and that she had full confidence in the Governor-General's decision. And although this incident led to reforms of the Australian Constitution, the Governor-General still has the power to appoint and dismiss ministers in Australia.

In 1977, she marked 25 years on the throne with a celebration called the Silver Jubilee. The Queen and her husband embarked on a three-month trip to 36 countries, a tour that further solidified the popularity of the Queen on a global scale. This was somewhat remarkable given that the Queen's sister, Princess Margaret, was going through a very public divorce after having some well-known extramarital affairs, many of which were publicized in the tabloid press. At the same time, the Queen was also dealing with the Prime Minister of Canada, a man who she has reportedly called a true disappointment. Pierre Trudeau was an anti-monarchy, pro-republican politician who publicly disrespected the Queen on several occasions, albeit in sometimes silly ways. The Prime Minister was seen dancing around behind the Queen's back when they appeared together and may have slid on the stairway banisters of Buckingham Palace like a hyperactive schoolboy. He even removed some royal symbols from the Canadian government during his term. In a more concrete and serious move, he pushed for the independence of Canada from the United Kingdom, by trying to bring the Canadian Constitution under the full control of the Canadian Parliament.

In 1979, as the conflict in Northern Ireland waged on, Admiral Mountbatten was assassinated by a bomb which was placed in his fishing boat by an IRA fighter. Mountbatten was the beloved uncle of the Queen's husband Phillip, a mentor to their son Prince Charles, the man who introduced the Queen to her husband, and one of the most important military commanders in British history. On the same exact day that Mountbatten was killed, the IRA ambushed British soldiers with bombs and gunfire. 26 of them were injured and eighteen of them died. This was the bloodiest act of the Northern Irish conflict and was considered a huge propaganda victory for the IRA. The bloody action fueled the ongoing war of guerrilla tactics and terror attacks for years to come. Mountbatten was given an honorable funeral at Westminster Abbey, the same cathedral where British monarchs are crowned. The Queen herself was of course in attendance, along with many members of the Royal Family, and royalty from across Europe.

On a more positive note, 1979 was also the year in which Margaret Thatcher became Prime Minister of the United Kingdom. Thatcher was the first female Prime Minister that the United Kingdom ever had. Like the Queen herself, Thatcher was known for her strength, which gained her the nickname "the Iron Lady". She would also become the longest-serving Prime Minister of the Queen's reign, having served from 1979 to 1990. And although some said there were tensions between the Queen and Thatcher, the two worked very closely together. Years later, when she looked back on her time serving the Queen, Thatcher said Her Majesty had "... a formidable grasp of current issues and a tremendous breadth of experience", which Thatcher believed to be deeply important to her decisions as Prime Minister. To this day, Thatcher remains a controversial figure: being both loved and hated by different groups of people with great intensity. And although some see her as an inspiration for women, her conservative and traditionalist viewpoints made her unpopular with many feminists and liberals. Her anti-communist, pro-business, and entrepreneurial values helped her to deepen the already significant relationship with the United States of America. This was especially true while the U.S.A. was under the leadership of conservative President Ronald Regan.

By 1981, another incredibly important woman was entering the world stage. This was the year that Prince Charles, the next in line for the throne, proposed to Lady Diana Spencer at the family home of Windsor Castle. They were married within the year, in a ceremony witnessed by nearly 750 million people worldwide. Princess Diana became extraordinarily popular all over the globe, as a fashion icon, for her charity work, and for her personality. The Princess may have been the most popular British royal family member of all time. Diana was at times outspoken and was often criticized for acting in non-royal ways. For instance, some said that her engagement with charity work was done out of the wrong motivation, such as self-promotion, and that it somehow tarnished the royal image. Some even called her a "loose cannon". The young Queen-to-be was still beloved and it seems that nothing anyone has said could shake her popularity. In fact, a BBC poll conducted in 2002 placed Diana as the third most important British person of all time. This puts her far ahead of the Queen herself, who ranked in at number 24 in the eyes of the British people.

The Falklands War broke out in 1982 when the Argentinian military invaded the Falkland Islands, which are under British control. The war lasted for 84 days and cost many hundreds of lives. This conflict was personally very nerve-racking for the Queen because her own son was activated to fight in the conflict. Although many in the government suggested that Prince Andrew be moved to a safer desk job, the Queen herself refused and asked that her son be allowed to serve as any other soldier would. He flew many missions in the conflict as a helicopter co-pilot, at times placing himself in great danger. Although the Queen would sometimes wake at night, worried about her son, she later indicated that she was very proud of what he did. The Falklands War ended with the withdrawal of the Argentinian military and the return of the islands to the control of the Queen.

In this period, with the growing global popularity of Princess Diana and a renewed interest in the Royal family in general, the tabloid news of England went into a frenzy, publicizing virtually any story that they could about the royals. These stories were sometimes true, sometimes totally false, and sometimes a strange mixture of both, but what mattered to the publishers was simply printing anything that sold papers. For instance, it was reported that the Queen backed the political opposition to Prime Minister Thatcher and that significant tensions existed between them. Thatcher herself basically denied this and the Queen's later actions toward Thatcher seemed to show her respect for the Prime Minister. The claim could have been based on some reality, and it is still hard to tell what really happened to this day.

From the mid-1980s onward, the royal family was being treated much more like celebrities than rulers in many ways. The press was even speculating on the extramarital affairs of the many members of the royal family, some of which were, in fact, true. The symbolic culmination of this strange period was when some young royal family members did a charity game show called, "It's a Royal Knockout". In this show, the young royals dressed in wacky, colorful costumes and participated in slapstick comedy games. After the filming, Prince Edward gave an annoyed interview with the British press, which he stormed out of after they seemed to mock him to his face. The whole incident was very surreal, and although the Queen and the other most important royals were not involved, it reflected very badly on the whole royal family and seemed to contribute to the general disrespect of the monarchy in general. But things would get worse for the royal family before they got any better.

Marking her Ruby Jubilee, or 40 years on the throne, Her Majesty said the year had been the worst of her life. By that time in 1992, her son Prince Andrew and her daughter Princess Anne were divorcing their spouses, something still considered disgraceful in the United Kingdom at that time. This is especially true since the royal family is supposed to uphold the Church's values and the Church frowns on divorce in general. The negative pressure of these incidents was only made worse by constant press coverage, selling the public on the royal soap opera. The anti-monarchy sentiment was continuing to grow at home as well. The monarchy was facing an unusual level of criticism, and the law was reformed so that Her Majesty would pay income taxes for the first time in history.

To finish the year off, Prince Charles and Princess Diana separated and the United Kingdom was losing their chance to have Diana as the next Queen of England. However, some say that this split was not exactly a surprise. Many believe it was the Queen who pushed Charles to marry Lady Diana in the first place, and that he may have never cared for her at all. For instance, in the very first appearance they made after getting engaged, a reporter asked the couple if they were in love. Diana responded "Of course" but Prince Charles added, "Well, whatever in love means". In 1992, the press obtained and released a secretly recorded phone call between Prince Charles and a woman named Camilla Shand, who Charles had previously dated. In a 1995 TV interview, Princess Diana described her marriage as being "crowded", and by 1996 they were formally divorced. Charles would later go on to marry Camilla Shand, but Camilla will not be named the next Queen of England.

In the year after the divorce, Lady Diana died in a tragic car accident while visiting Paris, France. The event shocked the world, as Diana was still massively popular globally, and Prince Charles had left the divorce looking like a villain. The royal family was criticized for not flying a flag at half-mast after the death, which was seen as a grave insult to the former Princess. This anger, coupled with an ever-growing anti-monarchy sentiment, seems like it should have ruined the royal family's reputation. However, the Queen managed to pull her people together. She addressed the world on the day before Diana's funeral and spoke of her love for the Princess, and her role as a grandmother to the children she had with Prince Charles. Even in this period, polls showed that the Queen had incredibly high approval ratings, such that even people who generally disliked the monarchy still had a love for their Queen. By the year 1999, the conflict in Northern Ireland was finally ending when the Good Friday agreement came into effect after it was approved by the Irish people.

By the year 2000, Her Majesty had been on the throne for 48 years, turned 74 years old, and showed no signs of slowing down. Though not quite as active as she once was, the Queen greeted the new millennium with the same stride and focus that she has borne for her entire life.

Chapter 5: Monarchy in a Modern Age (2000-2017)

In the age of the internet, the people of the world are more connected than ever before. News and communications seem to spread just as fast as they happen, and people are entertaining new ideas and ways of doing things as the world continues to shift and evolve. What does it mean to be a monarch in an era where self-governance and freedom are the ideal? For one thing, the Queen does not just represent the government of England, but also the Church of England. It seems to be in this role that Her Majesty has shined; as a symbol of the spiritual stability and traditions that create the identity of the English people. In a speech marking the year 2000, she said, "For me, the teachings of Christ and my own personal accountability before God provide a framework in which I try to lead my life." It seems that the people of the United Kingdom, and beyond, love the Queen for providing a moral rock to help them weather the storms of life. And in this role she has excelled ever since she first spoke to her people as a 14-year-old girl, telling the children of England to remain strong in the face of a Nazi invasion. She is undoubtedly one of the most philanthropic leaders of all time. As of 2012, she supported over 500 charities in the United Kingdom, helping them to raise about £1.4 billion.

In 2002, Her Majesty celebrated 50 years on the throne: her Golden Jubilee at age 76. It was in this same year that the Queen outlived both her mother and her sister. But if her mother is any indication of Her Majesty's hardiness, then she should fair very well, because the Queen Mother lived to be 101 years old! Refusing to slow down, she toured the world again to meet with her people on this 50-year anniversary. In fact, the number of people who turned out to see her was far past what most had predicted. In the next three years, the Queen underwent knee surgery and had a relatively small problem with her back, but she still continued her tradition of walking amongst her people in an uninterrupted fashion. That said, as time goes on Her Majesty is gradually passing some of her royal duties to her son, Prince Charles, and the other members of the royal family. This has given her more time to relax and enjoy her hobbies. The Queen has always loved dogs and has had more than 30 corgis during her time as the Queen. She has also kept cocker spaniels and dachshund-corgi hybrids called "dorgis". She has also been an avid horseback rider for decades, although she likely doesn't do this as much anymore, due to her advanced age.

Prince Charles remarried in 2005 to Camilla Shand, the woman who seemed to break up his marriage to Lady Diana. This wedding was unique in many ways. First, it was the first ever civil, rather than religious, royal wedding. Secondly, both Prince Charles and Camilla were already previously divorced. Thirdly, it was announced that if Prince Charles becomes King, Camilla will not take the title of Queen and will be known as "the Princess Consort". There were fears expressed by some in England that royal people could not have a civil wedding at all. This is because the Marriage Act of 1836, which created the right to a civil instead of religious wedding, supposedly did not include members of the royal family. Most of the government dismissed these claims and the wedding went ahead as planned. But what does it mean when the King-to-be has chosen to have a non-religious wedding even though he will someday become the leader of the Church of England? The Queen herself stated in 2002, "Change has become a constant. Managing it has become an expanding discipline. The way we embrace it defines our future"

As of 2017, the United Kingdom is undergoing one of the largest changes in its entire history. Fears of immigration leading to terrorism, the cultural identity of England, and a general return to conservative politics led the people of the United Kingdom to vote in favor of permanently leaving the European Union. Although the exit of Britain, called "Brexit", is still being parsed out by Parliament and Prime Minister Theresa May, the consequences could be enormous for the royal family. The chaos of the moment is being seized by republicans in the United Kingdom, with both Scotland and Northern Ireland gaining a renewed will to get their independence from the Queen. If these movements went forward, Her Majesty would have ruled the British empire at both its largest and smallest geographical footprints. It would also mean that the balance of power would shift within the European Union since the United Kingdom helps to form an alliance of voting power within the organization. This, and the fact that the United Kingdom is the second largest economy in the Union, means that Europe itself will be deeply changed by this development. The Queen has remained, as usual, silent on the issue of Brexit but she is no doubt watching very closely. She is also likely to be talking to a select number of important people about what she thinks in private so that she can guide them on what to do next. This is the way in which the modern monarchy rules: by allowing the government to work mostly on its own while providing a moral compass by which others can make the important decisions.

Queen Elizabeth II has now celebrated 65 years on the throne: her Sapphire Jubilee. In 2017, Her Majesty has turned 90 years old. This is a first in British history, and only one of her many records as Queen. She is currently the longest reigning Queen of all time, the oldest monarch in the world, and the longest running head of state ever. And although the Queen has passed more of her duties on to Prince Charles in recent years, she has shown no signs of wishing to abdicate, or give up, her throne. Between her hardy family history and the advent of modern medicine, she could theoretically serve well past the age of 100. Prince Charles, the next in line for the throne, is already 68 years old and a grandfather himself. This makes him the longest running heir apparent in the history of the British monarchy. As the Queen and her husband get ready to celebrate their 70th wedding anniversary, they must be looking toward the future of their family, both with the pride of what they have accomplished, and the anxiety of an uncertain future. Or maybe Her Majesty feels no anxiety at all, she has after all graciously sailed through a whirlwind of storms during her time as the Queen of England. The Queen continues to fulfill her duties, making speeches to Parliament, presiding over ceremonies, answering letters from the public, and meeting with leaders. It seems the only thing that has really changed is that she no longer travels abroad as much as she once did, but she is still very hardy in mind and in spirit.

Chapter 6: Legacy, Family, and the Next King

Queen Elizabeth II has certainly lived a long and colorful life, and although she has always kept her politics private, the Queen's poise, humor, and even a bit of rebelliousness can be seen shining through in several stories about her. Of course, she will be remembered as a guiding light for her people, as a stable and steadfast beacon by which Britons navigate their world. And although she is a regal and reserved woman, there were times when she showed a bold and somewhat mischievous side.

In 1981, the Queen was riding a horse in a ceremony when an 18-year old boy ran up to Elizabeth and shot at her six times. Her Majesty remained very calm, controlled her horse, and was totally unharmed. It was later found that the teenager was inspired by the fame some had gained by shooting celebrities and world leaders. The police later found that he wrote, "I will become the most famous teenager in the world" in his diary. Luckily, it seemed that he didn't really wish to harm the monarch, as he had loaded the gun with blanks. The Queen was praised by many for her calm and collected response: yet another example of the Queen's composure under fire. The very next year, a man named Micheal Fagan climbed over the walls of Buckingham Palace, broke into the building, and wandered all the way into the Queen's bedroom. She calmly talked to the man, and then went out of the room to get someone to help her . She never screamed or showed any signs of fear. The Queen managed, as she always does, to resolve the issue with a minimum amount of conflict.

In 1998, the Crown Prince of Saudi Arabia visited the Queen at her home in Scotland. The Queen knew that in Saudi Arabia women are not allowed to drive, and have significantly less rights than men do. In a bit of mischievous trickery, the Queen offered the Prince a tour of the area. After the Prince climbed into the passenger seat of the Royal Land Rover, the 72 year old Queen shocked the Prince by getting into the driver's seat and starting to drive him around while making small talk. Then, seeing that the Prince was uncomfortable, she started driving faster and faster, ignoring his pleas to slow down and that she should watch the road. She simply continued chatting with him, driving as fast as she could, until she finished the tour and brought them back safely. After all, the Queen was a trained driver and mechanic in the British military. Undoubtedly, her actions must have made her views on the Saudi laws very clear.

At some point in the last decade, a guard at Buckingham Palace almost killed the Queen by mistake. Her Majesty was going for a walk around the palace grounds and gardens. This sounds very normal, and should have been, but it was 3 am, pitch black outside, and the palace guard saw a dark figure walking toward him. The guard readied his rifle, and yelled out to the figure. When the guard realized who it was, he reportedly said, "Bloody hell, Your Majesty, I nearly shot you." The Queen was totally un-phased and replied, "Next time I'll ring beforehand so you don't have to shoot me." This is just another example of her classically strong and calm nature. However, within that strength there is a healthy sense of humor that undoubtedly reflects the humble nature of this most amazing monarch. When a minster asked her how she was doing in 2016, she replied simply, "Well, I'm still alive anyway" and laughed. And while she is likely to live on for some time, the Queen will eventually pass the flame of the British crown to her family.

Her Majesty's reign has set a high bar for the next monarch and no matter what happens, the next ruler will be in charge of a constantly evolving United Kingdom. A nation that will likely be changed forever by Brexit and all the shifts that this will create. And though some think of the monarchy as a symbolic position, the monarch can still declare war on other countries and is technically immune from any criminal prosecution. The oldest son of Queen Elizabeth II is next in line for the throne. The 68 year old Prince Charles of Wales has been training for this honor for nearly his entire life, and has taken on more and more royal duties in recent years. A mature and educated man, the Prince is certainly qualified for the position. That said, Prince Charles will likely face some challenges because of his public image. His high-profile divorce from Lady Diana is still a scar on his record and could create doubt in his role as a spiritual leader of the British people. He is also seen as somewhat "stuck up" by many in England, in contrast to his mother's gentler demeanor. After Prince Charles, the line of succession moves to the first son he had with Princess Diana. Prince William is a hugely popular figure in the United Kingdom, achieving fame that is boosted by the love that many have for his mother. Prince William is only in his mid-thirties, and will likely not serve as King for many decades to come. He has ample time to grow into his future role as king, but will likely be a very popular one when he does. His marriage to Catherine Middleton in 2011 was a momentous event that only served to boost the fame of the young royal couple. William also is seen as a dedicated public servant, even returning to his role as search-and-rescue pilot before he went on his honeymoon with Middleton.

For now, the Queen still reigns supreme, and when she passes she will leave a legacy as one of the most popular Queens of all time. Her willingness to embrace and manage the challenges and changes of the world should serve as an inspiration to those who will follow in her footsteps. But it can inspire people on a much wider stage than that as well, and this is the Queen's true power: to provide a foundation on which to place the hopes and dreams of one's future. This is her true legacy.

Conclusion

Thanks again for taking the time to read this book!

I hope that you found this book about Queen Elizabeth II to be an insightful and enjoyable read. Don't forget to take a look at my other titles available on Amazon!

If you enjoyed this book, please take the time to leave me a review on Amazon. I appreciate your honest feedback, and it really helps me to continue producing high quality books.

Printed in the USA
CPSIA information can be obtained
at www.ICGtesting.com
LVHW012142030924
790069LV00029B/944